T0208448

The Big D

TINA TRUMBLE

authorHOUSE®

AuthorHouse™
1663 Liberty Drive
Bloomington, IN 47403
www.authorhouse.com
Phone: 1 (800) 839-8640

Published by AuthorHouse 03/10/2020

ISBN: 978-1-7283-5080-6 (sc)
ISBN: 978-1-7283-5079-0 (e)

Print information available on the last page.

Any people depicted in stock imagery provided by Getty Images are models, and such images are being used for illustrative purposes only. Certain stock imagery © Getty Images.

This book is printed on acid-free paper.

Ok Ladies, it's time to talk about those nasty subjects that we all **D**eal with **D**aily, and how we handle things **D**ifferently than men. This combination of **D**'s is just a collection of my thoughts and you may not feel the same way I do on certain subjects, but I am sure you can at least relate. If not, you will at least find it humorous, I hope.

1

Dressing

Ok, so we can't go everywhere in our pajamas. Sometimes, we just have to buck up and get dressed. I've seen quite a few in the grocery store wearing the fleece pajama pants. I've been known to do it myself, in the winter time. It's cold, you don't feel like going anywhere, but you have to get to the store for toilet paper, otherwise it'll be a shitty situation. I get it. However, kids school events, work, and family obligations require us to get dressed. Our clothes make us feel good. It is a way for us to express ourselves, or so I'm told. I hate getting dressed! I hate clothes shopping. Most of the time when I find something I like, it isn't in my size, its cut funny or it's too expensive! Regardless, we can't run around naked, so we have to get dressed. I'm one of those that loves the hand me down bags. I enjoy going through people's clothes that they are going to donate, trying to find something that will fit me or I can wear at some point. All the while hoping that my friend has better taste than I do. The problem I have is that I have always been really small. I mean, I'm short. Let's face it, we can't all look like runway models when we walk into work every day. We all can't be graceful in high heels. Some of us look like baby giraffes trying to walk for the first time. We all don't have hair that behaves. My naturally curly hair is so unruly, I leave in the morning with it fine, but depending on humidity and temperature, and it usually ends up in a bun by the end of the day. Most days I am happy if I can get out the door dressed, hair brushed, and teeth brushed. I've always admired the women who can do full makeup and hair, accessorize and match their outfits, and always look so well put together. The women whose hair is styled, makeup perfect, earrings, necklace, bracelet, nails done, you know what I mean. I like to blame it on the fact that I have to get my kids up and dressed, but honestly I just don't' have it in me. I never learned how to apply makeup the right way, I try, but mostly I am unsuccessful. My mother wasn't exactly the kind of mom that taught us girls that stuff. My sister, five years to my senior was very good at it. That gene skipped me I think, and always being her annoying little sister, she never thought to show me. Also, I've always had to work, I mean really work: split wood, mow, weed, farm chores, on top of housework and working outside the home. Putting together well-matched outfits, and having manicured nails is really just not me.

I do try. I try to put the outfits together at the store, or out of my closet. Some days, I admit I just caffeinate and hope for the best. I dress fairly modestly; I don't like anything low cut or high rise. Probably because, God did not grant me the cleavage to fill out those low-cut tops. My petite stature has made it impossible for me to wear anything long, it will drag on the ground. Mini-skirts look more like midrise instead because I am so short.

I dread events! Those times when you want to wear

something special. You really want to look nice, we all feel that way sometimes. I think about what to wear for days before the event, and pick something that closely fits my needs. Most of us have been taught, almost conditioned to not want to feel pretty, that thinking we are pretty is Vanity and Vanity is sinful. Also, I know that most of us want confidence, however there is a fine line between confidence and conceit. I feel that, maybe I am alone in this. Maybe no one else dreads dressing as much as I do. I fear the ridicule of other women, we are all so judgmental. Even if someone compliments my shirt, did they mean that or are they picking on it. For years, people have made fun of my clothes, my hair, how skinny I am, flat chested, big butt, and now getting old. Do these jeans make my butt look big? Do I have muffin top? Do these shoes look alright with this? Am I too old to wear this? I don't worry about it much, but it does develop a complex over time. We are all so cruel to one another. No one picks out something to wear because they want someone to say something negative about it. Women pick clothes that make them feel good about themselves, express themselves. If it's not something you would choose to wear then fine, but they did and that is their choice. Give compliments, not judgement. Be the girl who boosts other women up instead of tearing them down. Try it! Let's see if we can build confidence in one another. Try to give out three compliments a day. It might make you feel good, to bring joy to another. Perhaps we can slowly end how we look at each other with judgement.

2

Driving

Life would be so much easier if we could teleport like on Star Trek. I live in the country; it is about twenty minutes to work every day. That's not a horrible commute, many people have it far worse. I live in upstate New York, where winter lasts five to six months. The snow and ice covered roads make for treacherous driving conditions. That twenty minute commute could turn into an hour on a bad day. It's not just the work commute, living in the country it is hard to get to the store, doctors' appointments, dental appointments, grocery shopping, kids' sporting events, and so on. I feel like I drive most of my day. I practically live in my car. Being a single mom and working full time, sometimes pulling two jobs, and three kids who have to go to the doctor, the dentist, gymnastics, their friend's house, and so on having a car is vital. I have a junk car. It's broke more than it runs, which makes my life difficult. I am so thankful and lucky to have a friend that lives near me, whom works where I do, so I can grab a ride on those days my car is being difficult.

Traffic in my town is not like that of a big city, the closest thing to a traffic jam around here is getting stuck behind a tractor. Sometimes the occasional lawn mower driven by someone who lost their license, or a load of hay. However, when I have to go to the city, it is a source of stress and anxiety. The closest city is not large like New York City or LA, but it's still a bit much for this corn-fed girl. I know I am not alone in the fear of city driving, I know several rural raised women who find this to be a difficult task. Driving in unfamiliar territory is the worst. I try carefully to plan my route, and my return route, but sometimes GPS gives us faulty information and we end up lost, despite our efforts. I have improved over the years. I have taken my kids on trips to different places. I've conquered highways, thruways, and interstates. I get extremely nervous driving next to the big tractor trailer trucks, or in heavy traffic, but I've managed to do it each time.

Parking is another issue in the city. DON'T LAUGH. I have no idea how to use a parking meter. I tried once, ended up getting a ticket. If I have to go to the city it is usually for a doctor or specialist located at one of the hospitals. The hospitals usually have a parking garage, I have learned how to use these. My hat is off to those that have to drive and park in the city every day. I know that I could not do it.

It takes so much time to get from point A to point B. Most of us busy working Moms, whether single mom or a married one, get the majority of the leg work. For example, your child has a doctor's appointment at 10:15am, you go into work until the absolute latest point possible for you to leave and go get your child to take them to the appointment. You leave work, drive to school or day care, pick up your child, drive to the doctor, back to school or day care, and then back to work yourself, you skip your lunch to make up the time you missed, and work the rest of the day until it's time to drive home again. I have several female co-workers and friends that the majority of these appointments fall on them. If a child is sick at school, it is usually Mom that leaves work to go and pick them up. As much as society has changed over the years, our "female" roles have essentially stayed the same. I'm not saying that the "Dad's" don't do anything or that even in some situations this may not be the case. I'm stating that in my situation this is the case and the case for most women I know. Most employers are not sympathetic either, regarding missed time, so this adds even more stress on the working Mom.

It isn't so much the driving sometimes, as it is about the other people on the road. I see it all too often, someone pulls out in front of me, only to stop or turn a hundred feet or more down the road. Another one of my favorites is the one that passes me when I'm driving slowly because of weather conditions, and then I pass them a mile or so up the road in the ditch. Everyone seems to be in such a hurry, and we all are! It is so important that we slow down, and pay attention. That means get off your cell phone, leave a few minutes earlier, and try to be as courteous of a driver as you are a human being.

Driving is a privilege. I am so thankful my father taught me how to drive. Believe it or not, I know some people who have never had a driver's license. My own sister doesn't. I cannot imagine having to rely on someone else to drive me. As much as I hate having to drive so much, I am extremely happy that I have the ability to do so.

3

Dinner

Why do they have to eat every single day? Whether you have kids or a partner, most of the cooking falls on us gals. We try to budget and plan our meals, trying hard to keep everyone healthy and happy. Even though most households require two working partners to function, the meal making, grocery shopping usually is carried more heavily by one party. In my situation as a single mom, and even when I was married is that I am the one that does the shopping and the meal preparations. Once I get home from work, it's time to think about dinner. If I haven't the forethought to get something out of the freezer, then I have to drive to the store to get something quickly. I'm usually very good. I like to plan out what we are going to have. Usually I do a two week menu, as I get paid bi-weekly and this makes money tight. The hardest part is when you ask what they would like you to make and they say the same things "I don't know." Or "I don't care." Then when you make something, they complain about it the whole time, picking at it as if it were going to attack them. It is a very frustrating situation. I've tried the "Make it yourself: nights that just turns into more of a mess for me to clean up and lots of wasted food. So, it is just easier and a lot more cost effective to just do it myself. If they don't give me input, I do what I think they haven't had in a while and make the choice.

The other thing I find is that eating healthy is so expensive. It is very cost efficient to eat box macaroni and cheese with hot dogs every night, however it is not very good for you. Fresh fruits and vegetables are expensive. It's almost as if America's obesity crisis is economically driven. We poor people can't afford to eat healthy, that was a joke, don't get offended. I do grow a garden, but I have that skill set, many people do not. Yes, there are food pantries out there, but I save those for people who truly need the help. My kids and I manage.

Eating out is something that many families do, that mine only does occasionally. I would say we eat out less than ten times a year. Some families eat out that many times in a month. When I was married and the kids were very young, it was once a year, for my birthday. It isn't that I don't enjoy eating out, it just that it costs so much money. I enjoy cooking as much as I complain about having to do it each and every day. I like to try new recipes. I love holidays and having everyone over to enjoy a big meal. Cooking for my family is an expression of my love for them. I just enjoy to do most of my cooking on the weekends, when I haven't been working all day. It is most fulfilling when I've had the time to prepare something special.

It is impossible to please everyone. We all have different tastes. I like my food spicy, it's a little too much for guests and my youngest daughter. My older kids share in my love of jalapeños and extra hot food. The spice isn't always taboo, people do enjoy my chicken riggies and enchilada pasta. I'm not much of a beef or pork eater, I prefer chicken. Although my daughter loves seafood, I am allergic to shellfish. The absence of shellfish, beef, and pork in most of my recipes makes it hard to keep a diverse menu. Then of course, there are always the preferred vegetables; potatoes, corn, etc. My kids aren't as picky as most. They will try vegetables that they haven't had before. My son once got into a trend where he was exploring wild edible plants. I find this fascinating. There are plants that grow literally everywhere that we can eat. You should really research the subject before experimenting thought, it can be deadly to eat the wrong thing.

My family is really not into eating breakfast, my son and I like coffee. My oldest daughter does not like any breakfast foods, she will eat left overs from the night before's dinner. I see Mom's in movies cooking pancakes and a huge breakfast before the kids get up in the morning, I'm lucky if I can sneak a quiet cup of coffee in while I sit trying to wake up before I get them up for school. I would love that idyllic scene, but does that really happen in real life? It doesn't happen in the lives of anyone I know. However, we do have dinner every night at the dinner table. Every one sits and eats together for dinner, and we talk about our days. Most of the time, the kids are picking and arguing with each other, but I do love that our family comes together to eat daily.

4

Daughters & Sons

I've been truly blessed with a son and two daughters, each one of my children are unique and perfect in their own way, that doesn't mean they don't drive me crazy. Since the day I found out I was pregnant for my son, my life was for him. It continued and followed with his two sisters. I try so hard to give them a good life. To protect them from the evils of the cruel world. Honestly if I can get them into adult hood without needing too much therapy. I think I've done ok. I've heard the quote "Behind every great kid, is a Mom that thinks she's doing it all wrong." this is so true.

Currently my son is a teenager. He is surly at times, he never wants to wake up in the morning, spends countless hours in his room playing video games. He rarely does any chore that I give him, each day is a battle to get his homework done. He seems very distant, sometimes I worry that this is a consequence of the divorce between his father and I. He hates school, but who didn't at fifteen? He doesn't turn in assignments. It is NOT that he lacks intelligence. That kid is smarter than most adults I know. It is simply that he just does not want to do it. He will do as little as possible, meeting the bare minimum requirements, and that drives me nuts. I've done research and this is a very common lethargic phase that many teenage boys go through. I know that he will get through this phase and will become whatever he sets his mind too. His intelligence and artistic abilities are surpassing average, he has a lot to offer the world. He is hysterically funny, we play lots of jokes on each other. He loves to antagonize his sisters, driving me a bit mad at times. We are a team, and when the chips are down I can always count on him to make the right decision.

My eldest daughter is a kind, sweet, quiet girl (until she is angry). She gets very frustrated with her brother and sister. She'll take their harassment until she's had enough. She reminds me of myself in that respect. She's a huge help to me, does chores, gets great grades, makes good choices, and I can genuinely say that I have no doubts or worries that she will continue on her path until she reaches her goal. I'm sure that she and I will have disagreements over time, but we will work them out. The only thing she and I disagree on is keeping her bedroom clean. She is unorganized, and a bit flaky at times. She tries very hard to please every one, she always tries to keep the peace between her constantly arguing siblings. I appreciate her gentle spirit and loving heart. She and I laugh a lot together, and I feel at times that I put too much responsibility on her, because I can count on her.

Then there is my baby girl, she is the baby in the classic stereo typical role. She is highly intelligent, athletic, energetic, and sassy. She is a great source of entertainment to our family. She is always busy. She's young, too young to see what her personality type will be, but she is stubborn, so I am sure she will be successful in any path she chooses. Her pre-teen attitude is fiery. She does have a kind, empathic heart, and a great sense of humor. Sometimes she takes things too far, and gets extremely emotional. She has intense feelings. One minute she's fine then one little thing goes wrong and she's upset. This is typical for most preteen girls. Although her older sister never went through this phase. Every child is different and I try very hard to help her work through her everchanging hormones.

Every mother feels like they aren't doing enough, or didn't make the right choices. We constantly worry about our disciplinary tactics, the rules, being fair, and trying not to show favoritism. Basically, I think we all just do our best and hope they turn out alright. I remember when all three of mine were in diapers, and how hard it was to keep track of the feeding, changing, and sleeping schedules. Everyone used to tell me that I'd miss those days, I don't. I cherished those times, the toddler times, and am even enjoying the teen and preteen times. It has always felt like it was us against the world. They know how much I love them, and that I will do whatever it takes to protect them. We've seen some hard times, we've seen good times. They understand even if they get disappointed that I can't afford to buy them something that they want, that if it something they truly want, I will find a way. They are spoiled in a sense, but not the typical type of spoiled. My youngest wrote an essay once for Thanksgiving, she said that her family was "rich" because we all love each other. She is right, and I am truly blessed to have my children. Being a mom is the only thing in my life that I am completely proud of.

5

Dieting

Ok, I'm going to just out right say it, I've never been one to sugar coat my words, WE ARE ALL BEAUTIFUL. There is no perfect image of beauty. We are all led to believe that unless we are tall, skinny, with big boobs, and perfect hair that we are not good enough. That's a bunch of bologna! I'm not one for eating all white meat and organic vegetables, or even exercising on a regular basis. My life style does not allow for that. I'm far too thin, my nerves eat the junk I put into my body before my stomach even has a chance to digest it. However, I know several gorgeous women who are in constant battle with their bodies. They try everything known to man to lose that extra weight. I know several ladies who have had surgery either successfully or unsuccessfully to lose the excess pounds. I'm not saying that obesity is healthy or even that I am a picture of dietary health. I am saying healthy is beautiful. If you are going to diet to lose a few extra pounds and get into a healthy lifestyle good for you. I do not have the patience to diet. I like food way too much. I love cheese, pasta, burgers, fries, deserts and all the things that are not good for you. I don't have time to exercise, but I'm very active and have three very active children. I don't make time to do it. I like walking in the spring and summer, but in the winter I hibernate indoors. My hat is off to the ladies who can go to the gym every day and eat salad. Kudos to you all that take the initiative to make yourselves feel better about your bodies.

I often wonder if everyone feels fat. I know I'm not fat, but when I look at myself in the mirror I see imperfections everywhere. For example, I have a small pocket of fat on one side of my C-section scar that hangs lower than the other side. Big deal, right? Well, to me it's a sore spot, a spot of self-consciousness. All the sit ups in the world won't fix it. I also have a fat butt and thighs, saying I feel this way often gets me in trouble with people. I know some people that struggle with their weight very seriously. I have sisters that do. This doesn't change the image I have of myself. I truly feel that we are all shooting for this idea of perfection that is unobtainable. That being said, dieting and exercising to be healthy is wonderful. Making yourself miserable and denying yourself the pleasure of a hot fudge sundae is inhumane.

We are not meant to be cookie cutter. Each one of us is unique. I think all women can agree, no one is more critical of us than we are of ourselves. I know just about every one focuses on their own flaws. Even the girls we think are completely confident, have their own little voice inside their mind that points out their flaws.

Dieting is great, if you are doing it to be healthy. Starving yourself to lose a few pounds, is just torture. Another one of my favorite lines is "Life is short. Buy the shoes. Eat the cake."

6

Divorce

Let's face it, no one stands on their wedding day thinking that they will be divorced someday. I did, I knew it wasn't going to work. We used to joke about it actually, he'd refer to me as his "future ex-wife". I already had our son and was pregnant for our eldest daughter. I knew he didn't want to marry me, but I wanted to be loved so badly I wouldn't admit that it wouldn't work. I wanted it to work and I believe he did too. We were young and foolish, made lots of mistakes. I'm not going to dive into the raw details of our marriage and why it didn't work. It was mutual fault, mutual resentment, and it just didn't end well.

Whether the love is gone or not, divorce is an awful ordeal. It's almost like a death. A death of a relationship, a severed tie. The dynamic of your relationship with the people in your partner's family is changed forever. No matter how long your marriage or long term relationship was, there are certain aspects of it that were good. Enjoyable moments, inside jokes, family dynamics that are learned over time, memories, and countless other things. It's difficult to maintain a friendship after the marriage/relationship ends. I was not able to do that. There was too much anger, hurt, and resentment. We do not speak, we text. Only in regards to our children. If there is a situation that needs to be have visitation changed or a child illness. There is no such thing as a civil conversation between the two of us. His family however, are amazing. I've always loved them, they love my kids and have always been there for them.

Starting over is hard. Many things are different after a divorce. Friends side with opposite parties, relationships change, and some people withdrawal not wanting to get involved, even if you are just trying to maintain a relationship with them and not trying to pull them into the middle. They find it easier to just avoid the situation completely. What makes this so difficult is that not only are you losing the relationship you had with your partner, you are losing the relationships you had with their family and friends.

Someone has to move, I chose to do that with my kids and my dog. That meant having to get all the basics again. Start over completely with kitchen items, towels, bedding, furniture, etc. Some cases the opposing partner can be generous and allow you to take what you need/want. It takes years to build up all your "Things". Things you don't even know you miss until you happen to look for them and realize, "Oh, never mind." It can be a very lonely time.

Making the decision that it's over is very difficult, many couples such as in our case try the counselling sessions. More often than not, the damage has been done the hurt, resentment, and anger are just too deep to overcome. Many times we blame ourselves for the failure of the relationship, some people want to put the blame on the opposing partner. The latter is easier, of course, but at the end of the day, in our quiet mind, we all know that it takes two. Sharing the "blame" for the dissipation of the relationship takes courage, and ultimately leads to forgiveness and the closure that we all need.

7

Dating

We all want to love and be loved. Whether you are 18 or 88, no one wants to spend their life alone. There is a whole industry dedicated to dating. I tired, after the divorce. Let's face it, thirties, three kids, mediocre income, I'm not exactly prime dating material. It's so hard to start over with someone. To trust again, to allow someone into our little protected place. Especially since we've all been hurt. It's never easy. We have this expectation of perfection imprinted into our brains. Too many Disney movies, or just too much television in general. We want it all. Many of us realize that our expectations are set too high, so we try to rationalize, compromise, and many find true happiness.

If we could have a partner that wanted to have a relationship built on friendship, honesty, loyalty, trust, common values, and goals of building a life together, we would be happy. But in order to find a partner, we have to date. I see it like picking out a used car, I don't have much experience but I do have female friends. Used car lot, test driving one after another, doing research, asking around for the best deal, and finally choosing one HOPING it isn't a lemon! I see it too much, it works out for a while, until it doesn't. There is an inside joke my friends like to use about having a broken "picker", this is to say your man picker is broken.

Then there is the matter of dealing with the "ex" or "ex-es", no one comes with a clean slate. We all bring luggage into any relationship. It's not easy. Relationships are hard work. Social media brings a whole new modern complication into the works. Worrying about hidden messages, checking their phone, I cannot say I'm immune to this. All I can say, from my own experience is that if there isn't anything to hide, then why hide it at all. Girls if you suspect something bad enough to go through your partner's phone, where's the trust? Why are you hanging on to someone you don't trust? Where is the value in the relationship without trust? Express your concerns to your partner, if they respect you enough they will be honest.

Kids add a whole new level of complications to a dating relationship. How will your children react to your new relationship? How long should you date before introducing the kids? What if your kids don't approve? Then the relationship works out, there are more complications. Your new partner will never be their parent. What if you don't agree on disciplinary measures? If your new partner has children as well, how will the blending of the family work? What are the guidelines? There is no easy way to do this. It gets hard.

After all is said and done, no one wants to be alone. We are all just looking for love. There are books, websites, and lots of therapists that make a lot of money on the human nature to be loved. Dating is difficult, but if in the end you find someone that you can build your life with, then it is completely worth the efforts.

8

Disease

There is nothing more terrifying than disease or serious illness. No one is immune, everyone has to accept it. Either ourselves or someone we love will get diagnosed with a disease at some point. My father was very sick with emphysema and COPD for many years. It was very difficult watching him suffer and to see his health fail over time. Several trips to the hospital, lots of appointments, more close calls than I can count, until ultimately it took his life. Dealing with someone you love being sick is so difficult. It weighs heavily on our hearts and our minds. Having a child with an affliction brings more heart ache than words are capable of describing.

Living with a serious illness or disease in your life makes the day to day life nuisances seem trivial. We often complain, myself included about the little things that annoy us. It's Monday, work issues, the weather and other normal complaints seem so trivial. The moment that your loved one is diagnosed with a serious affliction, those annoyances disappear. The illness is now the center of your life. Your days become less of scheduled events, and to do lists, and more of doctors' appointments and tests. Schedules become focused on medications. Life is altered.

It is exhausting, especially for the caregiver. Often times, one member of the family bears the majority of the load. Usually, this person is happy to care for the ill family member. It is so important that if you or your family find yourselves in this position that extra attention is given to the care giver. They will get burnt out if they don't get a break. They could develop their own health issues, that could be ignored because of lack of time to address them. I have seen this happen, for example a daughter caring for her ill father spend countless hours in the hospital, still went to work every day and cared for her own household. Often missing meals, losing sleep, and neglecting her own health needs. She had a heart attack at a very young age, now she is the one that needs to be cared for. Just remember, disease and illness affect all of us. Try to lend a helping hand, if you can. Even something as simple as calling to check if the family needs anything at the store or making up a meal to bring them can be a big help. A little goes a long way, and is often appreciated more than you know.

We would give anything, do anything to take the pain away from our loved one. We would take it onto ourselves if given the choice. Life isn't fair. It is heart wrenching and devastating. Life isn't fair. It ends to soon, and we often take our health and the health of those we love for granted.

9

Death

We've all lost someone. When someone you love dies, there is a hole in your heart that seems endless. The pain does not go away, yes it does get easier. Even time cannot heal the wounds death inflicts. You make room for the pain, grow used to the empty feeling. As the days go on without your loved one, the tears stop coming. Or a moment, a song, a smell, something happens that you wish you could pick up the phone and call them, but then you realize you can't. The tears fall again, the pain in those moments feels as fresh and raw as the first day. We all know that whomever in our lives is gone, they would not want us to be crippled by their loss. Some people deal with their grief and are able to move on, everyone deals with things differently. There is no right or wrong way to grieve.

I lost my nephew. We grew up together, he was more like a brother to me than a nephew. We were not far apart in age. He was my friend, I loved him dearly. His unexpected death ripped a hole in the hearts of so many people in our family. His life was cut short, and I never had a chance to say goodbye. His death still affects me to this day, it has been over ten years. I talk to him at times sitting down by the lake on my lunch breaks. I still cry.

My father died after a long battle with several illnesses. He had strokes, heart attacks, COPD, emphysema, cancer, and other contributing factors. Dad was a hardworking and good honest man. He taught me a lot in life. Although his death was expected, and actually a blessing to end the suffering he endured, I selfishly still wish he was here. There are so many times, I would just love a hug from my Dad.

Recently, I lost my dog. It was horrific. The person that hit him did not stop. He was a small dog, and it is possible that they might not have even known that they hit him. I was very distraught. I had that dog for fifteen years. He was my friend. Through thick and thin. I will miss him always. Losing a pet is like losing a member of your family. To true pet lovers, it can be devastating.

I've had too much experience with deaths of young people lately. It saddens me. People who had their whole lives ahead of them. It is so tragic. Suicide, overdoses, and accidental deaths are a daily reminder for us that we do not know the struggles of others. We should be kinder to one another, stop being so judgmental of one another. Life is hard enough on its own.

Death is forever. We always think we have time, but sometimes time runs out. I try hard not to leave things unsaid. It is important that even when arguments are happening, that the ones we love know that we love them. It only takes a second, a blink of an eye for something to happen and the chance to reconcile or talk it over is gone forever. Live like you're dying, because technically, we all are.

10

Depression

Depression, yeah we all get down sometimes, but when it becomes overwhelming, it's time to talk to someone. I have had to do that myself. Like I've said before, I come from a pretty long line of traumatic events. I have anxiety and depression. Living with it and maintaining a sense of normalcy in a world where mental illness is scoffed up like a joke. It physically hurts at times, my neck, my back, headaches, stomach upset, and diarrhea, inability to sleep, to eat, so nervous that all I do is shake or cry. I wrote a poem about anxiety I'll share at the bottom of this section, basically it feels like treading water in the middle of the ocean during a storm.

I know, I'm not alone in this. I've talked to lots of women in my life over the years and several of them suffer from the same affliction. It is not an easy thing to deal with. Lots of times the medications that are prescribed for such disorders have very serious side effects and a whole new set of symptoms develop. It is crucial for your own sake to be honest with your physician and talk about any new or worsening symptoms you might have. Counselling has been the key for me. I did not want to go at first, I did not want to admit that my depression was something

I couldn't handle. "Of course I'm depressed. Look at my situation." Was always my excuse. I was in a difficult marriage, then a difficult divorce, raising three kids, and struggling financially. It wasn't until I lost a bunch of weight and was unable to sleep at night that I realized the physical aspects of it. I decided to deal with my depression.

I think it is pretty normal, the more people that I talk to, the more I realize that several people deal with anxiety and depression issues. There is a stigma attached to it though, like the "things we just don't talk about". I think this is what needs to change. People need to stop thinking that you are "crazy" if you suffer from a mental illness, it does not mean that you are "insane." You are certainly not alone.

When the storm comes it is usually unexpected, sudden and violent. Waves of despair crashing over me, tossing me side to side, and pulling me under. I fight for each breath, praying I can survive, and at times wishing it would just take me. Treading water in the middle of the ocean, no land in sight. No life raft, no rescue crew. There is just me in the black, deep, night, storm raging, and still I fight. When it is over, I cry, exhausted and fatigued. Continuing to tread water until the next time.

The voice is the worst, coming from the quiet parts of my own mind. Saying all the horrible things that no one wants to hear. The one that reminds me of every painful thing in my life. The one that reminds me how unloved I really am. Screaming inside my head so loudly I feel almost as if it were its own presence. Words, whispered in the dark, frightening images when I close my eyes. Bringing me back to the worst points of my life. this voice brings me to the eye of the storm. Assuring me that I am unloved, broken, worthless, nothing.

And yet I am, I remain treading water in the middle of the ocean.

I wrote this at a time in my life when simply being alive felt like treading water in the middle of the ocean. It does get better. The sun comes up each morning, and with it the promise of a new beginning. I've felt the hopelessness that depression brings. I do know. I do understand. You are not alone.

11

Drugs & Alcohol

No matter who you are, where you are from, what economic status you hold; drugs and alcohol have touched your life in some way. Everyone has to deal with themselves or someone they know living with addiction at some point. It has become an epidemic in our new world. There is a difference between the occasional drink at the bar and alcohol becoming a part of your life. I have dealt with and continue to deal with alcohol having an everyday effect on my life since I was a child.

I grew up with an alcoholic brother. One never knew when and if he was going to come home, and what to expect when he did. It was a tumultuous time. He more than once knocked over the Christmas tree, it was weekly arguments with my mother and father. Even though he was much older than me, he would even fight with me. It affected who I would invite to my house as a child. It affected what I would accept as "normal" behavior throughout my adult life. I lived with an alcoholic, I drank a lot too. I bartended because it was an easy way to make money. It becomes a lifestyle. It took many years for me to realize, I did not want that life.

I have friends and family that live with drug addiction.

I've been lucky that I had enough fortitude to stay away from drugs. It does not take away, seeing what it does to people. I've been robbed, lied to, and cut out of people's lives all in the name of drug addiction. It is very sad. Too many people lose themselves, who they truly are, and the good things they have to offer the world by scrambling their minds with the sweet disconnection from the REAL problems. I believe and stand true in the belief that all people have good inside them. I try to understand and the hurtful things they do to obtain their next fix. I pray that they find a way to fight through it and become whole without the need for drugs in their life.

I try, and it is hard at times, to give a hand up not a hand out. If I see someone struggling, I try to find a way to help them. Rehab isn't the answer for everyone, neither is church. They need to find a reason to stop. All the influences in the world won't matter, if the person does not recognize that they have a problem. Sometimes, all it takes is an understanding ear.

There is a big difference between abuse and addiction. As long as you are happy in your life, it's no one else's business. Do your thing, hurt no one, especially yourself. Don't let it consume you. I've watched as people whom I was once very close to become strangers. I have had to sit back and watch as people who I love, destroy themselves. Even when they know it is a problem, it is nearly impossible for them to stop. They will do anything, say anything, hurt people just to get what they believe they need. What they really need is love. What they really lack is self love. If you know someone who is battling an addiction, love them, not enable them. Help them see their own worth. Give them hope.

12

Drama

Some people love the drama, some people hate the drama. Most people say they hate the drama, but create the drama. Even as an adult, arguments break out amongst friends. At times I feel like a time warp and everyone is a prepubescent teenager! My girls are in Middle School they deal with drama daily. I don't participate, and encourage them to do the same. If it does affect my life, I like to deal with it quickly and move on.

Some people call eventful lives "dramatic". Not everyone's life is easy going. A lot of people struggle daily, myself included. Just trying to keep their heads above water, while getting pounded down by life's never ceasing stresses. Some people choose to post their lives on social media. I am guilty of this occasionally myself. I usually come to my senses and delete my rants. Truly there is something good that happens every day. You just have to look for it and try hard not to focus on the negative.

Over reacting and crying out for pity and attention is really just a way for people to feel heard. Everyone wants to be heard and understood. Explaining everything to everyone is not necessary. I've learned this because I've done it. I used to feel the need to explain to everyone, everything. I did this in hopes that people would understand, that I would get some kind of validation for feeling the way I did. The truth is NO ONE cares. I did not need their understanding, approval, or verification. The only person's approval you need is your own. If you can look in the mirror and like yourself, that's all that matters. Only you truly know what a situation or life event has done to you emotionally. Only you can heal yourself.

The key to a drama free life does not exist. The best we can hope for is the tools to emotional deal with the drama that comes into our lives fairly and intelligently. There will always be people who don't like you, and those you don't like. Just be you, do you, watch out for you and focus on the good things. There is no need to create issues in other people's lives for revenge or to make them look bad. I have heard it said that it says more about the character of the one gossiping (spreading/creating drama) than it does the other person. A very true statement, something I have always heard, if someone says that so and so said blah blah blah about you, why not ask them, what did you say? Why did that person feel comfortable enough to say that about me to you? We can never know conversations that take place in our absence, but we can choose not to contribute to the drama by simply not playing into it.

13

Demons

We all make mistakes. It's whether we learn from them or not that makes all the difference. We all have things in our past that we would rather remained there. When we open ourselves up to other people, we risk that our demons will be thrown back in our faces at a later time. It is simpler to remain superficial, talk about nice things like the weather and the latest movies. Most of us have experienced something we just don't want to talk about. Nobody has a clean slate, there are always things we wish we had done differently. But until someone makes time travel possible there is no way to go back and change things. Even if we could, would it really matter? The choices we make, and the things that happen to us, mold and define us. Even the bad things that happen to us, make us who we are.

Our demons haunt us in different ways, but we all have to deal with them eventually. Whether it be our jealous nature, or something traumatic we would rather forget happened, we all have parts of ourselves we aren't proud of. The times that my demons like to come knocking, I like to remind myself that I wouldn't be who I am if things had been different. Also, my success rate of surviving difficult times is one hundred percent successful so far.

Talking myself through these difficult times is not easy. Sometimes I go weeks lying awake in bed, with my demons terrorizing my mind. Things I have done, that I could have done differently. Things that have happened to me, that I could have handled differently. Whether it is your own mistake or a trauma you have experienced, we all have our demons. It is in our own quiet moments that they come to our minds. We have to deal with them one at a time in order to win over them.

The other demons of this world are those terrible people who just hurt others. I am a strong believer that there is a special place in Hell for demons that harm children. One can only hope that the pedophiles of the world live in a damned tortured place for all of eternity. People that hurt any living thing that cannot fight back are truly evil.

14

Danger

Alright, we are women, and for us dangerous situations are a bit scarier than they are for men. Whether it is walking through a dark parking lot or having a confrontation, we are not all physically equipped to deal with danger. I'm small. I know that as much as my attitude makes up for my lack in size, I stand no chance against a grown man. I'd like to think that I can hold my own, take care of myself, but truth is the whole hundred pounds of me would quickly defeated in a physical battle. I also lack the mindset for physical confrontation. My fight or flight mechanism in my brain will always take flight over fight. My anxiety levels are through the roof the moment I sense danger is imminent.

I've had my car break down on the side of the road and had to walk. All the while thinking to the horror movie I've seen. I'm a mouse, I know this, and I've been called this numerous times. I avoid confrontation. I play it safe. I don't take risks.

My kids scare me to death with their lack of fear. My daughters and son love ATV rides and swimming in deep water. I know for the most part there is no danger, but there is always the chance that something could happen. We can't live in a bubble. We can't avoid everything for the "What if's?" That would make for a very boring and uninteresting life.

Unfortunately, the world is full of real monsters. I've had too much experience in life to feel otherwise. My life experiences have forced me to develop the "What If?" mindset. It has caused me to have anxiety when the "what ifs" become overwhelming. Mostly when I am out of my comfort zone. For example, I went to Niagara Falls on the Fourth of July with my kids. It was extremely crowded. The traffic on the trip there was outrageous. There was road construction and I needed to merge to get into the proper lane, It was a dangerous ride, but then we made it. After checking into the hotel, we walked down to the park to see the falls. There were so many people. I was terrified of getting separated from the kids. Then we went on the boat tour. While standing in line I kept thinking, it's a holiday. This is a prime terrorist attack location and with all these people here. Think about how catastrophic that would be. Then on the boat, it was super crowded. I swear it was at max capacity. The boat started to wobble; all I could think is what would I do if it were to tip? I looked for the life vests, locating them and keeping an ever watchful eye on my kids. I clung to my girls' hands and the boat did steady. I was never happier to be off a boat in my life, as when we stepped off. I know perhaps my anxiety is more of an issue than actual danger, but I live with the constant what ifs and am always playing the scenarios out in my head.

Over thinking the danger can be exhausting. I do find this to be the case, however I also think that I have stopped a lot of potentially bad situations by having the "What if" mindset.

15

Dealing

We all have to deal with the cards we are dealt. Some have a great hand, some have a bit more challenging one, but we all just have to deal with what we've got. Sometimes dealing with daily life is over whelming. It can lead to our thinking that we are doing it all wrong. Sometimes we just feel like giving up all together.

No one can change your life but you. If you aren't happy, make the changes in your life that will make it better. It's a lot easier said than done, no one understands that better than me. Truth of the matter is, everyone is just dealing with life. Just like you, just like me. Everyone has daily challenges, those differ from situation to situation. How they deal with it depends on the choices they make. If someone is born into a situation, they have to deal with that situation until they can get help or are old enough to make choices to change their own life. NO one is truly stuck. That's the beautiful thing about life, we all have the ability to write our own ending even though our beginning is out of our control.

The deal we are dealt, the challenges we face, the choices we make, change us and mold us. Hopefully we learn the tools necessary to deal rationally and positively.

If we find ourselves not dealing well with situations, then we have to take the initiative to learn the tools in order to deal with things better. No one is stuck. You are not a tree; you can pick yourself up and create a better life for yourself.

How we handle the challenges that our lives bring is different for everyone. Some people deal with problems by facing them head on, some ignore them, some self-medicate. However, you deal with your life is your choice. You are free to choose but not free of the consequences of your decision.

16

Delusion

I am guilty of being a bit delusional at times. I like to think that everyone has the best of intentions. I like to feel that people are inherently good. This is not the case. Most people don't care about anyone else's feelings but their own. They lack empathy. It is easy to take things at face value, but inevitably it is delusional. Things are not always as they appear to be. Knowing this causes us to get either 1) get lost in the delusion of things 2) end up pushing everyone away.

Not everyone is out to get me. I know that. I have been hurt by those closest to me enough to know that I will no longer suffer from the delusion that everyone can be trusted. It comes with age, hurt, and experience.

There is also the delusion that everything is alright. We all have experienced this at one point. It is impossible for us to know everything that is going on in someone else's heart or mind. We may think everything is alright, but in reality, it is not. It is unhealthy to think that everyone has the same heart that we do. People may act out, and we are not sure how to take it. The biggest thing that we all need to learn is to take a step back from these situations. Try to see things from another perspective, don't be so delusional that we think we are always right.

17

Daisies, Dandelions, & Other Weeds

Every mother knows there is nothing more beautiful than a dandelion bouquet from your child. They carefully select each and every flowered weed in the lawn. They hide it behind their back and bring it to you surprising you with the most gorgeous smile you've ever seen in the whole world. Your heart melts and you wrap them in a great big hug. That's a peek into my most precious memories of my own kids. Those flowers would sit in a glass on my counter until each and every one was dead. I loved and cherished those more than any rose boquet money can buy.

Speaking of roses, why do we swoon over a dozen cut roses? If a guy buys us roses does it mean he likes us more than if he picked us a bunch of wild flowers? Honestly in my opinion, I think I would swoon more over a guy having the thought and ambition to stop and pick me a bunch of wild flocks or better yet a bouquet of daisies. I've always thought the whole buying flowers thing was over rated. If someone really wanted to impress me, they would either pick wild flowers or get something I could plant in the ground, something that won't be dead in a week.

I feel the same way about buying flowers for funerals or any occasion really. I think it's more of an honor to someone's life to plant something in their memory. The money we spend on funeral floral arrangements is absolutely preposterous. Yes, flowers are very beautiful and they smell fabulous. This is just my opinion and no one has to agree or disagree with it. To quote one of my favorite sayings "I'm just sayin."

Every Valentine's Day, I watch the floral delivery come into the office and I think the bouquets are beautiful. I always think how lucky the ladies that receive them are. I also have seen how much they are to order. They are really expensive. Guys if you really want to make me happy give me that fifty dollars instead. I will used it for something I need., like towels.

18

Dogs, Cats, & Other Beasts

Many of us have pets, more living beings to be responsible for. They are a part of the family and bring us great job. Besides providing companionship, pets need to be fed, watered, taken to the vet (more driving and more money), loved, and disciplined. I have a dog, his name is Pinyon. He is a rat terrier, not a large breed of dog, he's about the size of a large cat. He hates men, always has. He barks like crazy at every man he sees. He's nervous, even had a seizure once when my boyfriend gave me a hug. Pinyon is loyal, he loves the kids and I so much. However, he has bathroom accidents sometimes, has a grass allergy, gets into the garbage sometimes, and can be a source of stress in my already maxed out daily routine.

Our family rescued two kittens once, they were so little their eyes weren't fully opened. Someone had disposed of them, it was winter time, I couldn't let them freeze to death. I brought them in, cleaned them up with warm soapy water. Their eyes were hard crusted with infection. The smallest one that was found in the ditch was so sick he couldn't move. His eyes so crusted, that when wiped with a warm wet cloth, a bubble of pus formed and burst. It was disgusting. The kittens were very sick and dehydrated. We named them Shadow and Shady. Shady was in extremely poor health. He didn't even move, he just lay in one spot peeing on himself. I took them to the vet, they were given fluids and prescribed antibiotics. They were so tiny, they didn't even weigh a pound. I fed them kitten milk replacement with an eyedropper. Now they are both happy and healthy. They wrestle with each other and race from one room to the next. They are WILD! We have a spray bottle filled with water to discourage them from jumping on counters, tables, climbing curtains, the walls, you name it. They drive us crazy sometimes.

At one point in time, we had a raccoon. Yes, a raccoon. She was actually tame, we got her as a tiny baby. Raccoons are smart. Squeakers, was her name and she absolutely adore my youngest daughter and me. She would nestle in my hair to snuggle. She would play like a dog, but wanted to be pet like a cat. Strangely enough she was very clean, she went potty on a puppy pad, and actually loved baths. Knowing she was a wild animal and needed to know how to survive, the kids and I taught her basic survival needs. The kids taught her how to climb trees. She would follow the up then be afraid to come down. She literally had to be taken down. We taught her to swim, we bought her a small kiddie pool. We filled the pool with rocks and got cray fish and hid them under the rocks to teach her how to find food. She lived in the house, until she grew very large and then one day, she just took off. It was an experience that neither I nor my kids will ever forget.

Regardless of what kind of pet you have, they own a piece of your heart. Pets are like kids with fur, that don't talk back. I know sometimes, they get on our nerves and our house would be so much cleaner if they didn't shed, but we love them. We wear our pet fur with pride.

My dog of fifteen years was hit by a truck. It was devastating to our whole family. It was a grieving process, I still am not ready to have another dog. He was my buddy. He followed me everywhere. I miss his excited bark, every time I pull into the driveway. I still forget he isn't here sometimes, and think I need to rush home to let him out. Even though he ruined furniture and drove me crazy sometimes, I miss him so much.

19

Doors

Who hasn't pulled on the push door or visa-versa? I'm that type of graceful woman who walks into things, like glass doors. I bump into mannequins and say "Oh I'm sorry, excuse me." Then realize they aren't a real person and laugh hysterically. Ah yes, graceful, that describes it to perfection.

I always seem to be the one that the wind catches the door and I have to fight to pull it shut. My car door, because I live on a hill, loves to slam into me, especially when the winter wind is whipping. I either catch a door to the leg/foot or it hits me in the face. Why is it every time the door to my house is locked it increases my need to pee by a million? Or when I am carrying loads of bags of groceries into the house, and finally make it to the door, the damn thing is locked? Let's not forget about the bathroom door. If I go into the bathroom and shut the door, not even thirty seconds will go by and one of my kids is knocking or walking in needing something. If it isn't the kids, the dog is whining outside the door, or the cats are pawing beneath it. I'm not kidding. I get into the tub or shower, someone is knocking (if not barging in) on the bathroom door. Moms are not allowed to pee or take a shower in privacy.

Doors are figurative and literal. Doors of opportunity, some of us can recognize them, I'm not one of these people. I feel like I'm on a game show when a situation like this presents itself. *"You can choose Door #1, Door #2, or the secret super prize behind the curtain."* I make my choice, only to realize later, maybe I should have picked another choice. I always manage to make the most of the choice I have made. I tell myself the next time an opportunity comes I'll be better prepared, but I don't ever seem to be.

I like to think on the old saying "When one door closes, another one opens." Sometimes when we shut a door on a situation in our lives, it is difficult to keep the door closed. Just remember, there are very few permanent situations in life. If the door you need closes, open it it's a door not a wall!

20

Diamonds & Other Rocks

We see it in the movies, the big proposal, and the ring. We all aim for it. We fantasize about it, even buy our own at times. A gift of jewelry from your significant other gives our hearts hope of a commitment. It's symbolic. The circle of love, never ending. The truth is, it's just a rock. It doesn't mean anything if the heart of the giver doesn't hold the commitment promised. A promise broken makes that diamond as meaningless as a rock in the driveway.

I've never been big on jewelry, working with kids with special needs for many years, it was a hazard. It doesn't mean that I wouldn't love to receive some as a gift. I guess people assume that I wouldn't like it, because I wear it so rarely. My sister has a ring for every finger. She's got enough invested in jewelry to pay my salary for five years. I'm just guessing, but I'm sure I'm close. I don't have any of value, and have always thought of it as frivolous. I prefer silver rather than gold. I like small jewelry, nothing too big or flashy. I also think that onyx, emeralds, and rubies are more beautiful than diamonds.

The symbolism is what I find meaningful. I would love for someone to give me a gift that really meant something to them. Make a promise and keep it. It could be something as silly as a gum ball machine necklace, but given from the right person, with their heart in the right place, it would mean the world to me.

21

Dreams

Dreams of grandeur, dreams of success, dreams of a brighter future, we've all got them. Goals are different than dreams. Goals can be attained. You can take steps to make sure you reach your goals. Dreams are illusive. Dreams take miracles to come true. I'm a dreamer, obviously.

I encourage everyone to dream. There is nothing wrong with it, who does it hurt? As long as realize that it's a dream, and will most likely never come to fruition. I like to believe that miracles happen every day and dreams can come true. I set goals in life, different than my dreams. I like to leave the dream door open, just in case.

Dreaming about things you would do if you won the lottery, is a little more fun if you play the lottery, but a little pointless if you don't buy the ticket. Dreaming about having a different lifestyle is different from setting life goals to ensure your lifestyle changes. Setting yourself up with a retirement plan is better than just hoping for the best.

Then there are actual dreams, the little movies that play as we rest. Some say dreams are a peek into our subconscious mind. I think some dreams may be our minds way of working things out, however I really doubt there is any meaning to most of the silliness I dream about. One time I dreamt I was pregnant for a puppy... it was weird.

I've always enjoyed writing. I wrote a few books. Will they ever pay off? Who knows? That's a dream, but at least I left the door open.

22

Demands

We all have people who depend on us. Our plates are overfilled with demands placed upon us by our families, our jobs, ourselves, our partners, and society. The demands that all of us have varies from person to person. Sometimes it feels as if we are being torn in a hundred directions at once. It is impossible to meet all of the demands placed on us. We need to set boundaries, have obtainable goals to meet the demands that are placed upon us.

There is also nothing wrong with delegating. Pass a few errands off to your partner if you have one, make the kids do a few chores. Ask for help if you need it. Most people are happy to help and can understand that sometimes the demands of our everyday lives leave us over extended or double booked. The thing that bugs me the most is when our parental obligations interfere with working hours, and most companies just don't understand or make it easy on us to take the time off needed for fulfilling the needs of our children. They need to be seen by the doctor, the dentist, orthodontist, and work places need to understand that these cannot simply be done on our off schedules. When you work Monday through

Friday, morning to evening hours like most people, you only have a slight window to get in appointments.

The demands we have on us now are not the same as those of our mothers and grandmothers. We live in a different world than they did. Yes, at the end of the day our goals remain the same, but now there is so much more pressure to succeed. Pressure to handle it all, without a hair out of place.

23

Dusting, Dishes, & Dirty Clothes

Dishes are dirty every day. Confession: sometimes when my kids are at visitation with their father, I avoid cooking just so I don't have to do the dishes. Does this make me lazy? Probably does, but when you are constantly cooking for five, dishes are inevitable. It always seems to me that they are there, just when I finish, someone gets a cup of milk or warms something in the microwave to snack on. I've tried having the kids help with the never ending dishes, and sometimes they do assist, but I usually end up doing it myself. Once in a while, my boyfriend will wash up the dinner dishes. It's a nice gesture and much appreciated.

Dusting, does it ever stop? Tiny particles of dust, pet hair, and fingerprints are constant. I am not obsessive compulsive or anything, but I have a hard time relaxing when I sit down and see a dust web or try to put on my makeup in a water splashed mirror! Does anyone else not see this? Add to all this, the doggie nose prints on the window created from my dog watching impatiently for me to come home every day. I love the stainless steel look, but fingerprints show up much more than they did on the old white standard ones.

Laundry, oh the laundry that never ends. With three kids and two adults, if I don't do at least one load every day, it becomes an over whelming pile in the hamper that taunts me. Another confession, I don't mind washing, drying, and folding. It's the putting away the folded laundry that I can't stand. I seriously pile my clothes onto my dresser until sometimes the weekend, when I spend a good portion sorting through and putting things into the appropriate drawers or hang them in the closet. My kids love to take all their clothes they haven't put away and put them back into the hamper for me to wash again, just so they don't have to put them away. This drives me nuts!

Unless you have a maid or a self-cleaning house, these mundane, monotonous, mind numbing tasks have to be addressed. I know lots of women, like myself, that save the majority of the chores for the weekend. We work all day, come home make dinner, have to do that load or two of laundry, do the dishes, help with homework, and by the time we sit down its almost time for bed. Maybe in your situation your spouse or partner shares in these tasks. That's awesome, I'm jealous. I know that the kids should help more, but they are teenagers and getting them to do anything is an act of Congress. I just know in my situation, the majority falls on me, and I find these chores to be as inevitable and annoying as death and taxes.

24

Doctors, Dentists, and Other Forms of Torture

Our health is something that cannot and should not be ignored. If we neglect it, then something can manifest that we absolutely cannot avoid. Those yearly pap smears are vital. Mammograms are essential in early detection and prevention for breast cancer. Regular doctor visits can be the difference between life and death, at times. Dental health is another thing we like to avoid, but unless we want to be toothless, we need to keep up on it.

The yearly GYN appointment, scheduled so far in advance, I usually forget until the phone rings and I get the reminder call. We miss work to go into an office, lay half-naked on a table, have someone insert this thing that looks like something from the Spanish Inquisition into our most delicate area, feel just a little "pinch", and we're good for another year. I don't know about you gals, but I dread this. I feel so awkward. I know that it's necessary. I avoided it for years and ended up having problems that I couldn't avoid. I have ovarian cysts, mostly they don't bother me, but when they aggravate they can be very painful.

The mammogram process is just about the same, only

this time we are naked from the waist up. I'm a small woman, my Dad joked one time about me not needing a mammogram, because I didn't have any boobs. Having a very cystic body, I also have cystic breasts. Since I run on caffeine and nicotine my whole body is just one big white blur. The imaging doesn't take long, but there is always something detected on mine that leads to a sonogram. It's so odd having a stranger rubbing on your breasts looking for a lump. It's just weird or maybe I am.

The dentist is another inconvenient but necessary appointment we need to keep. I have bad teeth, lots of issues there, since I grind my teeth at night my back molars are gone now. Also, having been in a terrible accident as a child I have a partial implant. I went to the dentist weekly for years, having them attempt to do their best to repair the damage that was done from the accident. I think it traumatized me to avoid the dentist. I make sure my kids see the dentist regularly but admit I neglect my own appointments. Another contributing factor to me missing my own appointments is that I have to miss work in order to go. If you don't make time to go, like me, then sooner or later a cavity is going to erupt and you're going to be in a lot of pain. Nobody likes to go, lay in a chair, hold your mouth in odd uncomfortable positions, have instruments half choking you to death, and if you have any teeth sensitivity OUCH!

Moral of this is, it is so hard to keep up on our health as well as everyone else's in the family. Missing work to take the kids to the doctor is just a part of parenthood, but making time to go for ourselves we see as just inconvenient. You can't take care of anyone if you neglect yourself. Make the time to go, it is essential.

25

Devoting Yourself

Devoting yourself to your family, your job, your religion is a part of life. We almost all do it. Lose our sense of self after years of laundry, dishes, laundry, working, and raising babies. We devote so much of ourselves to everything whole heartedly that it becomes who we are.

I know women that devote themselves to their professions, in the name of trying to do well for their family. Only to have lost all the precious time they were at work and their children were being cared for by someone else. It is modern women's hardest choice. There is no right answer to this.

Those women who do choose to stay home, their job is their home. We all know that keeping up with a house is a full -time job. Especially when there are young children present. It is sometimes more economical, given day care costs, for one parent to stay home.

Devine devotion. I don't feel the need to go to church every Sunday in order to maintain a relationship with God. I will not get into religion or put my beliefs out there, I will just say that the women who devote themselves to service in the name of their religion are troopers. It is thankless and often ill received for "messengers of the word". If you have touched one life, God bless.

26

Disasters

Reports of disasters around the world are tragic, we all wish there was something we could do to help. Everything from earthquakes to mass shootings take place daily. I could not even watch the reports on the tragedy in Sandy Hook on the news. It was too sad for words. I empathize with people who are witnesses or relatives of the victims. My heart breaks for them. Many people can just watch the nightly news and remain unaffected by the disasters that unfold around us. There is nothing wrong with being detached nor is there anything wrong with empathizing. I do believe that we as a society are becoming more and more desensitized to these disasters. We see it all too much, television, social media, ads, everything is in our faces all the time.

Then there are the mini disasters, just life throwing us curve balls. Flat tires, power outages, storms, miscellaneous home repairs, just mere inconveniences in the big picture of things. But, in the moment, it feels like the worst possible thing that could have happened. Don't get me wrong. I get discouraged! My washer decided that it had washed and spun out its last load, now I have to buy a new washing machine. Add that on top of the never ending list of things we need, and bills to pay. It's just another thing. No, certainly a broken washing machine is not the end of the world, but when you have laundry piling up for five people and no way to get it done, it certainly isn't the most wonderful news.

27

Dermatologist Recommended

Wrinkle creams, anti-aging serums, makeup, and medical procedures; all things us women buy in order to avoid the inevitable. We all age, some more gracefully than others. We spend millions of dollars yearly on this industry. Does any of it really work? Can we really turn back the clock? It is a nice idea, but in all honesty a pretty farfetched one.

I am not innocent of not buying into this delusion. I buy the wrinkle filler and moisturizers. I try every new product there is. I have these "eleven-lines" between my eyes. I call them my "WTF" lines. That shit runs deep. I've seen the tape that you can wear to bed that will "train" your muscles and will lessen the depth of these lines. I don't have the patience for this. I have the smile lines, and the crow's feet. Add to all of that the big dark bags under my eyes, and as you can see, I am picture of self-confidence.

I know women who have had the Botox injections, good for them, they look fantastic. I cannot justify the cost of what to me would be frivolous and ultimately vain investment. I couldn't do it for myself, good for the girls that can. The facelifts, tummy tucks, and breast implants are for other people not for me. There is nothing wrong with women having these procedures to make them feel better about themselves. I'm just saying that for myself, I can't afford it, and even if I could I don't really care about it all that much. I feel that aging is a part of life and no matter how hard we fight it; it is coming and it sure beats the alternative. But, at least you'll be a better looking corpse than me. Growing old is a privilege denied to many, be grateful for your life.

28

Disagreements

Everyone handles disagreements differently. Some people yell and scream until people bend to their will, some people just walk away and do not engage, some people mull it over and over in their heads and approach differences of opinion in a very methodical way. I usually end up walking away from a disagreement only to kick myself for the things I did not say. I have never been well equipped for arguing. It makes me nervous. More often than not, if something happens that I disagree with I bite my tongue until they happen over and over and finally I explode. I try to avoid this if I can. I try really hard to not hurt anyone's feelings or do something that might upset someone, but no matter how hard I try, soon or later someone is upset over something. Like the old saying goes "You can't please them all."

Yes, the best way to handle a disagreement is to talk it out. To allow the other person's point of view to be heard, to try to empathize with how they are feeling, and reach a compromise. I hardly ever see this happen in real life. What I do see, is that when people disagree they stop talking, avoid one another until they are over it or they just hold a grudge.

We can't agree all the time. It is impossible to agree with everyone. We can agree to disagree, and handle the matter with civility and respect.

29

Determination

Being stubborn is one of the only things that has kept me going this far into my life. I have a very determined side, determined to succeed where others have told me that I would fail. I remember once my ex said I wouldn't last a month without him, look at me still going. I work hard, I set goals, I do the best I can, I fail, I fall, I pull myself together, and try again. The greatest thing about being determined to have a better life, is that every day you are fighting. Fighting for a goal. Yes, there are a lot of obstacles that get in the way, but if you stay determined, stay focused, and keep your eye on the goal, you will get through it. Every step forward, even the tiniest one, gets you closer to where you want to be. Some days it feels like the battle is lost, that doesn't mean you've lost the war. Find the determination to pick yourself up, and live to fight another day.

If you are determined to do something, you will get there. It may not come as quickly as you would like, but if you continue with determination and do not give up, you will achieve any goal you set for yourself.

30

Deluge

Real life example: You just got out of work, it is payday. You go to the bank because you need to stop at the store and get some groceries before going home. You pull into the local Walmart and there is barely any parking available. Into the store you go, trying to hurry because you haven't even been home yet. You do need to use the bathroom, but you can wait. You hurriedly go up and down the aisles trying desperately to remember what you need. You had prepared a list, but again left it on the counter at the house. Navigation your way through the crowded store, you keep getting behind all the slow people who don't have a care in the world. Skip aisles to avoid the people who have blocked both lanes to stop and chat. Finally feeling that you have gotten everything that you absolutely need, you head to the check-out line. You browse through the lanes looking for the shortest line. Every single open lane has at least five people in front of you. There are so many people in the store, everyone just like you has just gotten out of work and are trying to get what they need and get home, but at the moment you are so frustrated you begrudgingly pick a line and wait.

Hoping your bladder does not explode before you pay for your groceries.

Am I the only one who experiences this? The never-ending flood of people at the grocery store. It doesn't seem to matter which day of the week I pick or what time of day neither. Let's all try to make it a little easier on everyone else, if you happen to run into Suzie from high school in the pasta aisle, pick a side.

there are also those times when we hit a rough patch in life. More than once I have experienced weeks where everything that can go wrong will. There is really no way to avoid these patches, just hold on and pray for better days. It can't rain forever.

31

Dialect

I don't know about you, but I get really annoyed by people who pretend to be something they are not. I find it very annoying, for example, when teenagers and even adults from my area (literally the middle of nowhere upstate New York) talk like they are from the city. Not that people from the city talk differently, but they often use terms and sayings used in music, movies, or tv shows. They use terms that I need to look up in the Urban Dictionary. Get real! Talk normal it drives me insane. I actually have explained to my kids that talking like that could be considered extremely offensive!

Every area of the world has terms and phrases that are indigenous to that area. For example, in the midwestern United States, soda is called pop. Simple things like areas, roads, stores can be referred to as something other than what they are actually called. I find it fascinating. I know the FBI has developed a linguistics science around this, being able to track down criminals from phrases and terms used in their writings or speaking.

I'm not one to commonly complain about swearing, I swear all the time. Friday is my second favorite "f" word. I did steal that from a t-shirt. The cussing does not bother me, if used in the proper context. Trash talk does bother me. I get very uncomfortable when people openly and more disgustingly talk about their lives in the bedroom. I also dislike name calling and putting people down.

Ladies, especially young ladies, clean up your language. You are beautiful, intelligent, and funny you don't need to talk dirty to be sexy. You already are.

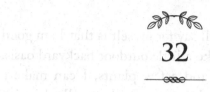

32

Decorating

Whether it's Christmas, Halloween, or any other holiday I've always admired the ladies that can decorate. This gift was not bestowed upon me, I put out everything I have and hope for the best. I try. At Halloween, my favorite holiday, I put out my scarecrows and pumpkin decorations. Then I drive by people's homes and see how awesome they look and I feel inadequate. The same goes for the Christmas tree. Some people have the time and energy it takes to make sure every ornament is in the right spot. I don't have time for that. I'm happy as long as I have a few of my favorites (mostly things my kids have made for me) on and it looks semi festive. I'm really not a "girly-girl" all those wonderful qualities I admire in other women seem to have skipped over me completely.

I enjoy other people's decorating. I love walking into someone's home and seeing all their matching furniture, accessories, and what not. I admire people who can, first of all afford to decorate like that, secondly that have the ability to put it all together. I know what I like, but I usually don't have the money to spend on decorating. Any extra, yeah like that exists, always goes to the kids or for the next thing we need on the list.

The one thing I will say for myself is that I am good at gardening. I can make a little outdoor backyard oasis. Given the right tools and a few plants, I can make a garden anywhere. This I can do, and I actually do enjoy it. I have really fixed up the little place the kids and I have to make it look nice outside. It's amazing what you can do with a little mulch and some hostas.

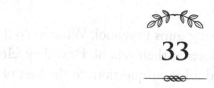

33

Difficult Conversations

At some point we have to address difficult topics. Whether it is having "the talk" with our kids or having to tell someone news that we know they are not going to be happy about, we've all been there. I don't know about you, but I have the conversation about ten times in my head before I actually have the conversation. Going over and over every response to every question or comment I can imagine them having. I dread these conversations.

I recall having one of these conversations with my father when I was young. I had to tell my Dad that I was smoking. I had been caught, I knew the conversation was coming and tried to avoid. I got yelled at, but what was worse, I had disappointed him.

I have had to have several of these conversations with my kids. We are very open with each other. The sex talk wasn't the worst conversation we've had to have, neither was the divorce talk. The one that I recall being particularly difficult was the one about the school violence occurring. Sending your kids to school shouldn't be a source of anxiety or fear. Violence in our schools is something we all really need to talk to our kids about. This conversation between myself and my children we talked about kids bringing guns to school. What to do if there was an active shooter at their school. How they felt about it and I answered all their questions to the best of my abilities. These are such dangerous times we live in.

Discussing drugs and alcohol isn't an easy one to have with the kids either, but it is necessary. Like I've expressed, we are very open with one another. I know they will have to deal with peer pressure, and I hope I have given them enough tools to help them through it. Most importantly, I have assured them to call me. No matter what, no matter where they are, what they have done, I will always come and get them. I would rather be woken up at 3am for a ride home, than have anything happen to them.

34

Digging Up Dirt

Never doubt the investigating abilities of an angry woman. We can do research and pull up every dirty little detail that you've tried to hide. We will wait for the perfect moment to have the big reveal. Women in general are passive aggressive, building up all our anger until a big blow up. I've tried to stop this. When someone used to say something rude to me, or hurt my feelings in some way, I would bite my tongue. I would let things go and go and go some more until I explode. I am working on being proactive about this, and trying to discuss things that bother me before it gets to the point of no return.

The truth is, if you are looking for dirt you will find dirt. What good can you do with the dirt? Most of us don't utilize our investigative abilities for the good. We use them to find out all the dirty details of our ex's new fling or our current partner's ex. It's a bit ridiculous actually. We all have a past. Most of us make mistakes. Who are we to judge? Hey all for it if you want to dig up dirt on your neighbors but I'll stick to my own yard.

35

Distraction

My mind is constantly going. As I am trying to fall asleep at night, I am thinking about all the things I need to do the next day. It is a constant never ceasing list of "to-do's". Bills that need to be paid, chores that need to be done, groceries that need to be picked up, appointments that need to be made or kept, things I have to do at work, etc. I always have something going on. Being in my mind is like having thirty open apps on your phone, it slows down the progress of everything and nothing ever gets completed.

Who else is easily distracted? What was I doing? Why did I walk into this room? What was I saying? I start cleaning one room, or begin a task, only to be interrupted and then have my focus shift to something else entirely. Often feeling like I accomplished nothing, because nothing is complete.

I make lists. Lists do help me focus. I have to write the simplest tasks on the list. My kids always joke, that if it isn't on Mom's list, it doesn't happen. Trying to juggle everything, all the time, I find the lists helpful when I remember them.

Another way that I have learned to battle the constant

distraction is to block out chunks of time for certain things. For example, on a Saturday I will clean for one hour straight, then I will chunk out fifteen minutes to check my phone or take a break, the next block of time is designated for reading or writing etc. This way I can focus on getting as much done in the designated time as possible. Multi-tasking is great, but sometimes it leaves things incomplete. Chunking time helps me to stay focused on one thing at a time.

36

Dining on a Dime

We all wish we could eat out every day, but as awesome as that we be, we can't afford it. I rarely eat out. I brown bag my leftovers to the office every day for my lunch. I am not one of the gals that gets asked to go to lunch daily with the co-workers. I think I do well budgeting my food. I feed five people as inexpensively as I can. My secret weapon: Casseroles. Casseroles go several meals, left overs can be taken for lunch the next day and makes the grocery budget stretch just a little bit farther. Yes, meals like pasta, scalloped potatoes, baked macaroni and cheese, chicken and stuffing, and soups are hard to make during the week. If you plan correctly these meals cost less than twenty dollars to make and can feed five people at least four meals (lunches included). I make a couple large meals a week, I encourage them to eat the leftovers at least one night a week. It helps.

Still it is appalling how much food we throw away! It could feed a whole other family. Every week I buy only what is on the list. I always ask each member of the house if they need or want anything specific. I am always met with the "I don't know" and "I don't care." I remind them of that when they complain about what I put in front of them.

Truth be told, I spend more money on food than any other expense in my home. I shop the bargains, I clip the coupons, I try everything to save money on groceries. The biggest problem I have is the waste. I think we all throw out more than we wish we did.

I garden, this does save on produce costs. However, canning and processing your own spaghetti sauce really isn't an economical choice. A can of spaghetti sauce is less than a dollar and it costs more than that for the jar and lid. It doesn't make sense to say that canning your own vegetables is to save money, it is more an art form or a lifestyle choice.

37

Diversity

We live in a mixed society. Blended families, different ethnicities, sexual orientations everything makes us each different. Being open minded is essential in getting along. Everyone is unique and in a unique situation. How boring would it be if we were all the same? Unless you live under a rock, you will have to deal with people that are different than you are.

People have the right to their own opinions and lifestyles. We all need to get a grip on this situation. I see too much of it daily. People pushing their ways onto others, it's not ok. Judging people for the way the choose to live, not okay. Don't believe in gay marriage? Don't get one. Don't like smokers? Don't smoke. Everyone has their right to live and be the way they choose to be. It isn't our job to teach morality or family values to anyone but our own families. Even then, our children will grow and be able to decide for themselves. Stop trying to make a cookie cutter society, when we live in the largest cultural melting pot of the world. Seriously. Learn some tolerance.

38

Damsel in Distress

Okay girls, save yourself. No prince is coming on a white horse to whisk you away to a fairytale life. This is reality. You aren't going to meet a millionaire who happens to be your soulmate by accident.

Since no one is coming to save you, save yourself. Learn how to fix your own plumbing, teach yourself to be independent. Trust me when I say, know what you bring to the table and don't be afraid to eat alone. I know from personal experience that it is a lot better to earn your keep on your own, than have someone say "you wouldn't have that if it weren't for me".

It isn't easy facing the dark and cold nights alone. It is hard. Life is hard. We've built up this image in our minds that we need to be rescued. Truth is, that no man really wants a needy girl. Be the kind of woman you would want your daughter to be. Be proud of the steps you take to better yourself. Every small step toward a better life is a step in the right direction.

39

Down Time

Free time, time that has nothing scheduled, everything is done. Does this exist? It happens from time to time, although rare. When you get this time, what do you do with it? I have a list of things I want to do, because it happens so randomly, I often forget the things I put off to when I have some free time. It helps to write them down. I have a list of movies I want to see, books I want to read, places I would like to go, and things like that. I don't get it very often, but when I do find myself with some free time, I often write. Writing for me, helps me put the things going on inside my head and my heart onto paper. Giving these feelings and thoughts words, brings them to life. Not everyone likes doing this, but that's ok. Find what works for you.

We are given twenty four hours each day. Eight are usually spent working, count in two for travel time, eight for sleeping, two more for eating, what are we left with? Not a whole lot. Add in the time we spend cleaning, cooking, doing laundry, helping with homework, and other daily tasks we are left with minutes instead of hours. Minutes we usually spend sitting in front of a television, trying to relax our minds.

I would hate to be at the end of my life, and realize that all the down time I had, I spent in front of a television or scrolling through my phone. I want my life to be filled with adventures. I want happy memories with my family. No one talks about the time that we all sat in the living room watching television. It is a goal of mine to get off my butt and get out into the world. Have those adventures and make those memories.

40

Due Date

There is nothing longer than the last trimester of pregnancy. Time stands still, hours seem like days. It feels as if your baby will never arrive. You miss your body, you would love to see your feet again, sleeping is uncomfortable. Honestly everything is uncomfortable. The baby sticks its little feet under your rib cage, or rolls just right onto your bladder. Oh yes, the joys of pregnancy.

My poor niece, first baby is overdue. She is in such pain daily from the very large baby in her belly. All of that will be over soon, and in an instant, she will have relief and joy at experiencing the birth of her baby girl.

Seriously, is there anything more painful than child birth, other than a man having a cold? Honestly, they say you forget the pain. No, no I remember the pain well. It is agonizing, excruciating, and seems like it will never end. Then, the pressure and the release. Hearing that first primal cry melts your heart like no other sound.

41

Desire

We all want to be desired. We look for someone to love, someone to love us, someone to look at us like we are the most beautiful creature on the Earth. Everyone feels this way, yes, even men. The problem is, how do we keep that alive once the initial "honeymoon" phase of the relationship is over?

Date nights are essential for keeping the love alive. Communication is key to any relationship. Try new things, build something together. Whatever works for you and your relationship, do it.

Surprise him/her with notes, try to be playful. Make your partner your best friend. Appreciate each other, be grateful for the little things. Do these things and the desire will be there.

If you find the desire slipping, which it will, and I think is extremely common and normal. Please, do not seek attention elsewhere, let your partner know how you feel. Try spicing things up a bit in the bedroom, I don't know. I am no expert on love and romance, I just know from my own experience that time tends to wear on the relationship. Sooner or later you look at that person like they are just another mouth to feed and person to pick up after. All the while, we wish that the desire for one another was still there. So, my advice, try.

42

Due Diligence

Like it or not, sometimes we just have to wait. We have to give things a chance to unfold they way they are supposed to. It isn't easy, in this modern world we are conditioned to seek instant gratification. Unfortunately, most things in life take time. I am not a patient person. I don't have patience for fast food. Even though I know that sometimes we have to give things a chance to work themselves out. We have to sit back and allow the pieces to fall where they may. I am horrible at this.

When faced with a situation that must allow time to see how things will work out, I tend to over think. I play out each possible scenario in my head trying to predict or will an outcome. My efforts are fruitless, we just have to wait. You can however use this time wisely. Perhaps there is an outcome you don't want to have, then what? Well, you could use the time to prepare yourself in case that is the outcome.

I am an overthinker, I play out each possible outcome, and how it could play out over time. Often causing myself more stress and anxiety over situations that I have absolutely no control over what so ever. Giving things time to play out, is a difficult endeavor that many of us, including myself are totally terrible at.

43

Daily Grind

An unguided hand reaches aimlessly for the incessant buzzing. In the dark, fumbling to find the snooze button on the alarm clock. Finally, hitting it and just as you drift back to sleep, there it goes again. A glance at the time shows that you really need to get up. The kids need to get ready before the bus, you need to get ready for work. God forbid that it snowed last night. Your feet hit the cold floor, sending goosebumps all over you. You hurriedly wake the kids, pack the lunches, brush their hair, "Are you really wearing that to school?", followed by the eyerolls and slamming doors. Ah yes, the morning routine. You need to look halfway presentable to go to work, so you hurry through your routine, interrupted by the hundred questions. "Where's my backpack?" "Did you sign my permission slip?" "Where my …..?" The bus beeps and the kids rush out the door, leaving your "I love you. Have a good day!" unanswered. You drive to work, do your daily routine, eat at your desk, finish out your day, go home, make dinner, help with homework, get everyone ready for the next day, do laundry, dinner dishes, and finally hit the pillow, Just to do it all again the next day.

The struggle is real. We women know this better than

most. The day to day, repetitive, exhausting lives we live. Our days are so routine, we go into auto pilot. I know I do. Throw into that the daily calls we need to make to keep in touch with our loved ones. There are just too many routine tasks that we do over and over again, day after day. We tend to take our routine for granted until something disrupts it.

44

Debt

It really sucks working just to pay bills Welcome to adulthood. We all work our butts off to pay our way through life. Most of us can't afford the lifestyles we want so we turn to credit.

Credit cards make our lives easier for the most part. We can buy groceries and get gas between paydays. Almost all our large purchases are bought through credit. Who has cash enough laying around to buy a house outright? Nobody.

The problem occurs when our debt outweighs our income. This comes from living beyond our means. We don't mean to do it, but the trap of minimum payments and monthly interest keeps us locked in a viscous cycle.

How do we get out of it? One step at a time, pay them down. Try to make more than the minimum monthly payment. I know that's impossible right? I get it. Try rounding to the nearest dollar to start out with. It's just a few cents difference, but over time will add up.

I am not an expert, but I do know a little on this subject. I refuse to have a credit card anymore. It makes things too easy for me. I have no impulse control for buying things. I won't even have an ATM card, I do have a prepaid Visa that I use. It helps me control things a lot better. I can only spend what I put on the cad. It does help.

45

Democracy

In our house, we run as a democracy. We vote on things to do, dinners, and lots of other things. However, like in our real government votes can be overruled by the higher authority(me). I like to honor the kids' thoughts and opinions on things. I also think it is important for them to have a voice in decisions. I am afraid that often, as parents, we over look the fact that our choices affect them. Moving, for example impacts the kids' and even though it may be the best and most economical choice for the family, it affects them considerably.

It is imperative to see all sides of the situation before making major decisions. Have everyone's opinion heard and considered. Realize that it isn't just our life, that we affect the lives of those closest to us with our choices. My father and my ex always had the "It's my way or the highway attitude", obviously with the latter I took the highway. My Dad on the other hand, was more reasonable, some issue could be debated and debate I did. So much so that it earned me a nickname, that I will not share, when I was very young.

Voting is our right in this country. I can't stand people who post pollical satire on fb without knowing the full story. The hate memes and jokes about our nation's leaders is all too present in our daily lives. In my OPINION, we should not share or like these posts. It draws negative attention and allows negative influence. How do we stop the corruption in government? Quit voting for crooked politicians.

46

Desensitized

With all the terrible news we hear daily, the violent movies and video games, the harsh realities of the world have desensitized us as society. There was a time when hearing an "f-bomb" in a public place would have raised eyebrows, now no one blinks an eye. We are overly exposed to violence and sex. It doesn't even bother most of us anymore.

Does anyone else ever think about the effects of this? I mean the long term, I'm not one of these that blames everything bad that happens on the television shows and video games. I do often wonder how it has affected us as human beings. We don't talk anymore. We don't write letters. Everything communication is via text, there is something lost in this. The tone, the sarcasm. Words on a screen are open to interpretation. It can lead to miscommunication.

Is this really how we want to be? How impersonal are our daily communications? I try to talk to my sisters at least once a week. I make it a point to not just text. Hearing someone's voice allows a connection to occur. If things are not fine with the person we can often tell by their tone of voice. This tone is lost in text messaging.

Believe me, it is a lot less time consuming to text than make a phone call. I understand that in our busy lives, time is precious. I like to think that face to face communication is best. Again, we are losing this and are becoming desensitized by just texting.

I am going to go out on a limb here and say that we are teaching our kids to be insensitive. Empathy is something that we are losing as a quality in people. Yes, we encourage acceptance for all kinds of people. Empathy is something different. Teaching our kids about the human connections, putting ourselves into someone else's shoes. We are teaching from a point of blind acceptance, instead of understanding.

47

Dishonesty

Everyone lies at some point about something. When someone lies to us, we lose trust in that person. Trust cannot be rebuilt in some cases. Sometimes it's like smashing a plate on the floor, gluing it back together, and ignoring the cracks.

There are the big lies. Infidelity, stealing, or other criminal acts. Then, there are the little lies, calling in sick when you really aren't. We are all guilty of some degree of deception. Fess up when you screw up. Don't lie about it, truth is it will only get you into more trouble. Chances are that people already know the truth. Guys, if she asks about it, she already knows. Kids, Mom knows a lot more than you think she does. She wasn't born under a rock, she had a life before children, and she probably did more crap than you ever will.

It would do us all a lot of good to have a degree of transparency. Although some things are just not anyone's business, so instead of lying about say "What do you want to know for?" I stole that line from a good friend and colleague of mine. Everyone doesn't need to know everything.

48

Delegating Duties

It is not easy for us to give up parts of our routine. The kids don't clean as thoroughly as we would have done ourselves. Coworkers don't do things in the same order as we would have. Partners buy the wrong brand of an item at the grocery store.

We give specific instructions, just for the person we are delegating the task to, to do it their own way. We get very frustrated by this and would rather take all the tasks onto ourselves without delegating anything. It's easier sometimes to just do it. We need to stop.

Stealing a line again from my friend "A problem passed on, is a problem solved" She is an extremely smart lady! I have learned so much from her over the years. The world gives us enough, pass on what you can. Teach your kids responsibility, make them do chores. They will screw it up, teach them how to do it correctly. It's ok.

We need to stop micromanaging everything. I am guilty of this myself. Our way is not the only way to do something. Being open minded about other ways of completing something might actually be beneficial. Never stop learning, be teachable.

49

Damp Squib

Have you ever purchased something that was supposed to make your life easier only to find that the product does not live up to its hype? A certain vacuum or washing machine that was supposed to make household chores easier? Even a cleaning product that declared it takes out stains, and really doesn't work as great as it does on t.v.? These products are damp squibs. They do not live up to their expectations. As I have said before, money is often tight for me so when I buy something, I expect it to work.

Recently I purchased a smart tv. I am sure that there is nothing wrong with the tv and I am just lacking in technological intelligence to figure out how to work it. I thought it would be easy. The advertisements show that this television is capable of doing all kinds of things. However, I can barely turn it on. Sometimes, I get so stuck I have to call to my son to help me figure out how to get to my favorite show. There are too many choices. It is an endless list of available shows, movies, and documentaries. I have no idea how to work the darn thing.

Don't even get me started about cars. They all have problems, they all cost money, and unless you have a good mechanic friend you are going to have to pay.

Bottom line, most things are not what they are made out to be. Everyone has different experiences with different things. I don't ever listen to the hype over the latest and greatest thing. The only thing I wonder is why are there advertisements for toilet paper? Who isn't buying this stuff?

50

Damned if You do, Damned if You Don't

It is so hard to try to please them all. It's impossible. I often think of a poem "Be a Lady They Said". Do this, don't do that, do that, don't do this. Dress appropriately, dress sexy. Curls are out, straight hair is in. Be natural, wear make -up. The list goes on and on.

It is impossible to win! If you try to do something, you face the harsh judgement of your critics, if you don't do it, then you face the harsh criticism of people who think you should have tried. The most absolute and only failure is the lack of attempt. You can't please everyone, so don't even try. Set your own goals. Believe in your own sense of integrity. You are the one who has to live with yourself for the rest of your life.

If life has taught me one thing it is this; you have to look at yourself every day and learn to like what you see. Everyone else is temporary. It is a sad but true fact. People move, people die, people grow apart. Our circle of friends changes over time, rarely we find people who are loyal and stay in our lives.

In the end, every day we make decisions and choices.

Options are endless. You're damned either way, so at least try to make yourself happy. Be genuine to yourself, because that is the only one who has to live with the decisions and choices you make.

51

Denial Ain't Just a River in Egypt

You need a partner not a project. A man will act right for the woman he wants. People change when THEY want to. You can't fix stupid. Don't settle for less than you deserve. Ignoring the red flags you see in the beginning will be the reason you leave later. Be honest with yourself.

That all being said, we all have lived in denial about something or situation. My check engine light is on, well it's not making any noise so it can't be that bad. I will only have one more drink, three hours and a karaoke performance later. Don't live in denial. Accept situations as they are, don't make excuses for your or someone else's bad behavior or choices.

I have lived it, you want things to be one way or another, and they just aren't. No matter how you dice it, slice it, mince it, or rinse it the situation is what it is. So, don't waste your time, know your worth and don't settle for less than you deserve.

52

Devine Intervention

We have all been at a turning point in our lives at one point or another. Everyone has struggled with life. It is in our moments of absolute desperation that we pray or turn to something bigger than ourselves to show us what to do. Something or someone to guide us. I have had several moments like these in my life, and I choose to believe that it is Devine intervention. At these difficult and dark moments God guides me to make the best choice I can make.

Not everyone believes in God, and that's ok. I just have seen in my own life how the power of prayer gives me strength. It does not take away my grief or pain, but somehow praying gives me hope. I know this is a little crazy, sense I do not attend church, but I believe that one's relationship with God doesn't have to be in a church. I think that God can see into our hearts and knows what kind of person we are. I trust that I am a good person.

God has manifested miracles in my life. At moments when I truly needed a miracle to help me through, something has come along and given me that little bit I needed to carry on. Often times through regular people. There are angels living among us. So, I pay it forward.

I help others when I can, expecting nothing in return. I pray for people who hurt me and hope that they find peace in their hearts. Normal people don't destroy other people, if someone hurts you, there is something wrong with them, not you. Pray for them to find healing that they need. Trust that there is a bigger plan, and believe that you have a role to play in it.

53

Don't Borrow Trouble

As hard as it is, don't borrow trouble. Try not to overthink things and worry about things so much. We have very little control of things as it is. Sometimes we take on more trouble than we have to and stress ourselves out even more. Life is full of these situations, and a very wise woman used to tell me all the time to not borrow trouble.

It is hard to let our friends and family members work out their own problems, especially if we have experience in the situation they face. We have to remember to give advice when asked for it, and not take on the responsibility to fix the issue for them.

Life throws us enough curve balls. Try not to attract them by having a negative mindset. By worrying constantly about what can happen, you miss out on what IS happening. We only get so much time, and life gives us enough trouble, don't borrow it on purpose.

54

Dynamics

We all play a role in our own lives. Everyone has a spot to fill, including us. This varies from our own family where we are the mother, to our original family where we are the sister, daughter, cousin, aunt, etc. Even within our work life, there are roles.

How we interact with one another and the standard behavior or method of reactions is different depending on whom we are dealing with. The dynamic of the relationships we have established determine our behavior in certain situations. For example, one holiday, not sure which one, we as adult children with our spouses sat at the dining room table at my parents' house. One of the kids did something, I cannot even recall what, and my father slapped his hand onto the table, and we (all my brothers and sisters) literally jumped and fell quiet. I laughed immediately afterwards regarding how we all reacted. In that moment we were all children.

Everyone plays different roles in each type of relationship we have. How we act is dependent on the dynamics of that relationship and the role we play in it. Take a moment to think about it. Would your coworkers talk to you in the same manner as your family does? No.

55

Decaffeniated What?

I drink way too much coffee. I know this because I account for how much I drink in a day by pots instead of cups. I know it is not great for me. I also know that I make The Gilmore Girls look like rookies. I am pretty sure that my body will still be moving two days after I die. I drink so much coffee because like many things in our lives, it has become a viscous cycle.

I don't sleep well at night. Therefore, I am very tired in the morning. I drink coffee to wake me up. In the mid -morning, early afternoon I drink more coffee for energy. My son usually has a pot waiting for me when I get home from work. This is my pre dinner energy. The energy it takes to jump into round 2 of my day. The evening laundry, making dinner and doing homework part of my day. I try to stop drinking coffee by 7pm otherwise I won't be able to sleep at all.

A good friend suggested I try decaf coffee. I about died laughing. What is the point of that? Decaf coffee is like snuggling with a prostitute. Doesn't make much sense. Like non-alcoholic beer. Just takes all the fun out of things.

56

Dinosaurs

I became an expert on dinosaurs, when my son was little. He was the only three year old I have ever met that wanted to be read Encyclopedias at bedtime. He learned about the different time periods, and the different creatures that walked the Earth during them. I found this information to be very useful in my work with Special needs children later. I could always reference the different types and explain more than the average person about dinosaurs and how they lived. My great nephew still refers to me as the Dinosaur lady. I too find it fascinating that these massive creatures existed and waked the planet like any other animal does today.

I stare in wonder at the exhibits at the museums of dinosaurs' bones. There is so much work involved in excavating the bones from the ground. The latest animatronics brings these amazing creatures to life. I don't know of many people who can't look on in a sense of awe. Can you image walking outside and seeing a creature as big as a bus? It's impossible right? But they lived.

My son's love of dinosaurs is shared by most young people. Now that he is grown the creatures hold a special place in my heart, because like them my little boy has gone through the phase of time and is now a young man.

57

Doorbusters

Since "Black Friday" is approaching it brought this one section to mind. Why do we stand in line the day after Thanksgiving, trying to save a buck or two? I refuse; absolutely will not after one experience I had years ago. Furbies were the rage for all the kids. I got up at 4am to go stand in line with my sister. She had a daughter and a step-daughter that absolutely had to have a Furby for Christmas! There were limited quantities, one per customer. We stood in line at the mall at K-B Toy store. There were several people already waiting when we got there. I remember thinking, "What did they do camp out here?' The store finally opened, and the first fifty people got the Furby. The clerk ran out just before my sister and I. I remember, my sister was furious. The product was available before Christmas and no childhood trauma occurred. They were the same price as the special "doorbuster" price on Black Friday. My years of experience has shown me that this is usually the case.

The other side of this is, why do we need to get that one thing so badly? What message are we sending to our kids? I realize that most of us try to make our kids have a better life than we did, but if that is all materialistic, is that really what we want? I come from a humble family and often struggle to make Christmas happen for my kids. It is just my opinion, but Christmas has become so commercialized. My love for someone should not be reflected in the amount of money I can spend on them.

I enjoy the little things about Christmas. Having often not been on the receiving end of the gift giving, I draw my Christmas spirit from decorating the house, making cookies and candy, and preparing a special meal for my family. Sure, I love getting gifts as much as anyone, but I feel that the holidays are more than just that.

To get back to the original point, if standing in the freezing cold and fighting the crowds on "Black Friday" is your thing, God Bless. It's just not for me.

58

Dancing

If you see me dancing, call me a cab, I'm obviously drunk. I have the moves of a tone -deaf hippopotamus. They say dance like no one is watching, this makes me laugh because I know how ridiculous I am. That's ok, it doesn't stop me from letting loose once in a while.

I admire the people who have moves. They appear to have the rhythm and don't look silly. And God knows I'm a sucker for a good slow dance. Nothing is sweeter than a man holding you close, your head on his chest. Twirling around and coming back in.

My favorite dancing is the kind that happens in the kitchen. Music blasting, cooking up a meal for my family and singing into the spoon. I haven't had that in a long time. It is good exercise and a great release to be silly once in a while.

So dance, every dance you can. Dance alone. Dance with someone you love. Dance silly, dance slow, dance to your own music. Smile because it feels good. Dance until your ribs hurt and you are so out of breath you're going to pass out. Because, there is far too much fun to be had by dancing to sit it out.

59

Dire Straights

I am sure you have heard the saying "The rich get richer, and the poor get poorer." I believe this statement to be true. Think about it, it is so expensive to just survive. Rent, utilities, food, gas, insurance, etc everything costs money. I don't believe everyone should be on welfare or that we should have a communistic or socialist economy, but we do live in a society that does not really foster growth.

Banks, for example, charge over draft fees for insufficient funds. Charge more money to someone who already doesn't have any. No, it is not a good idea to write checks without having the funds, but some of these fees are a bit ridiculous. ATM fees, charging you money to take your own money? Some ATM fees are over five dollars. It is a bit ridiculous.

Utility companies, charge late fees for late payments. Customers already are struggling to pay the payment itself. Yes, it does encourage consumers to pay on time, but sometimes I just have to shake my head at the fees and charges.

I am just complaining a bit, I struggle financially sometimes. It is not easy to make payments on time, every time. Most months it is down right impossible. So, I do what everyone else does. Look at the problem and try to find a solution. I do not feel that I have a spending problem, it's an income problem. Most households require two working people to make ends meet. I have tried working more than one job, and it is exhausting, but I have done it when needed.

60

Domestic Goddess

We are all the Queens of our own kingdoms. Each one of us is loved and admired by our family. Even though when we are still in Friday's pjs on Sunday morning because we just didn't have the energy to get dressed yesterday, we feel like the servants of the kingdom. Yeah, we are tired. We are overworked and underappreciated. But, in our home whether it's a palace or an apartment we rule.

There are many ways we don't even see how important we are. I look to my own mother, because it is hard for me to see my own worth. I think to her, how she held it together. How she cooked, cleaned, was wife and mother, it was different for her than it is for me, but I hope my kids someday look at me with the same admiration.

Our homes are our castles and we do have some control. We can choose to let the laundry go another day. No one will be naked or without clean clothes for a day. We can take a break and watch Lifetime movies all day on a Saturday. It's ok. Let the guilt of the dirty dishes go.

61

Diabolical

I used to think that everyone was inherently good, that there were good qualities in even the worst of people. Watching crime television and too much news brings me to the conclusion that there are some people who are just down right evil.

People kill their own children, throw them into the trash, bury them in the back yard, put them in a dumpster, or some other disgraceful place, like the child has no value or worth.

Criminals, terrorists, and boogey men are real. They walk beside us on the street, even scarier sometimes live in our own homes. You can not think that everyone is out to hurt you, but it is wise to have a bit of a defensive stance.

62

Double Standard

Ok, it is time for me to just say it. There is such a double standard against women. Women are criticized over every little thing. It's ok for a man to have several sexual partners, but if a woman does the same she's a slut. It is expected for a woman to work in the relationship, cook, clean, take care of the children, while the man works and comes home to relax.

The worst double standard I feel is the expectations placed upon women. Dress like a lady, but be sexy, don't drink, but don't be a prude. Don't be too fat, don't be too skinny. Be intelligent, but don't let on that your too smart. It's ridiculous I hope that I have taught my daughters that the only standard you have to live up to is your own. Expect your partner to contribute to daily duties and don't accept less.

63

Drained

At the end of the day, we all feel tired. Have you ever felt so tired that your spirit was tired? Like all life has been drained from your soul? It is the kind of tired that no amount of sleep can relieve.

Being in a constant survival mode is exhausting. Just trying to survive until the next break through, to get a breath of air. Life is a constant struggle, it is tiring.

You can't drink from an empty cup. If you don't take a little time to fill yourself up, sooner or later your will be empty. I know how hard it is to find time to do anything, most days I feel like I am in constant work mode. If you don't pick a day/hour/block of time to rest, your body will pick it for you.

Perhaps more importantly, fill your soul up. Do the nice things for yourself that make you feel pampered. Go to church, if that's your thing. Take a walk in the park. What ever it takes, to make you feel relaxed.

64

D. You all know what I am talking about

We have different parts than men, we are physically built differently. Our bodies go through puberty, men do as well. The difference is, when we women go through this we have the dreaded "curse" menstrual cycle. Cramps, bleeding, constipation, headaches, and hormone fluctuations are just the tip of the ice berg of the symptoms that come on us monthly. I have already touched base on pregnancy and there are so many books out there on that subject that I feel those changes go without saying. But oh boy, we all thought our period was so bad, just wait it gets so much worse.

Peezing, the wonderful sneezing and peeing your pants at the same time. Most of us tense up when we feel a sneeze come on, cross our legs, and hold our bladder as best we can. This is a very uncomfortable and not often discussed part of being a woman after child birth.

Another wonderful joy of being a woman is menopause. The mood swings, hot flashes, odd rashes, aches and pains more fun milestones in the life of a woman. What do men get to deal with in their midlife? Erectile disfunction?

Sex is often something we just don't talk about. There is a taboo placed on discussing it with anyone. Orgasms are the biggest stress reliever we can have. Stressed out? Get laid. You'll feel better.

65

Detoxify

We all put stuff into our bodies that we need to get rid of some times. We exercise, drink kale shakes, take vitamins to get rid of the toxins we have in our bodies. What about the toxins in our minds? Negative thoughts can be just as potentially dangerous to our health as eating fast food morning, noon, and night. Just as we need to detox our bodies, we need to detox our minds. We need to be just as devoted to healthy minds as we are to healthy bodies.

If you are plagued by negative thoughts, as I often find myself to be, we need to try to find something that works to break the cycle of negativity. I met a lady recently that told me to try replacing every negative thought with three positive ones. I am trying. I find it to be harder of an exercise than running a mile daily. (Which I would not do). But, if I could, I used to and think that running that mile was easier than retraining your brain.

I am hoping that the outcome is worth my efforts. I always practice empathy and forgiveness towards others. However, I am finding it pretty hard to use those on myself.

I also heard meditation helps, I tried that. I am constantly distracted by the things that I need to do. I have my writing, it seems to be a healthy outlet. Perhaps someone reading this feels the same way I do.

66

Don't Forget About You

It is in our nature to put our families and others before ourselves. Most of us are givers. The important thing is, as hard as it is to find the time to do the things that you enjoy doing, you really need to. I know better than most how hard it can be to juggle the job, the house, the kids, sports practice, games, doctors, dinner, and everything else. When am I supposed to find time to sit down and actually read or write a book? Well, I don't. I write in bits and pieces, here and there, hoping I remember where my train of thought was when I can get back to it again. The things is, I don't give it up, because that would be letting go of something that I enjoy doing.

Every one of us is unique. We all have our own special talents. We put so much into everything we do. Take time to pamper yourself. Make a phone call to an old friend. Go for a walk, whatever it is you need to do to focus on just you.

I lost myself, for a very long time, pouring every ounce of energy I had into everything and everyone else. Once I found myself alone, I did not know who I was anymore.

I am still discovering that. We are constantly changing, even though we don't see it. We lose our own identity sometimes, and it is important that we maintain that connection with our true self.

Printed in the United States
By Bookmasters

Printed in the United States
By Bookmasters